THE BEGINNINGS OF DEMOCRACY

NICOLAS BRASCH

Nelson Thornes

First published in 2007 by Cengage Learning Australia
www.cengage.com.au

This edition published in 2008 under the imprint of Nelson Thornes Ltd,
Delta Place, 27 Bath Road, Cheltenham, United Kingdom, GL53 7TH

10 9 8 7 6 5 4 3 2
11 10 09 08

Text © 2007 Cengage Learning Australia Pty Ltd ABN 14058280149
(incorporated in Victoria)
Illustrations © 2007 Cengage Learning Australia Pty Ltd ABN 14058280149
(incorporated in Victoria)

The right of Nicolas Brasch to be identified as author of this work has been asserted by him/her
in accordance with the Copyright, Designs and Patents Act 1988

All rights reserved. No part of this publication may be reproduced or transmitted in any form or
by any means, electronic or mechanical, including photocopy, recording or any information storage
and retrieval system, without permission in writing from the publisher or under licence from the
Copyright Licensing Agency Limited, of 90 Tottenham Court Road, London W1T 4LP.

Any person who commits any unauthorised act in relation to this publication may be
liable to criminal prosecution and civil claims for damages.

The Beginnings of Democracy
ISBN 978-1-4085-0196-2

Text by Nicolas Brasch
Edited by Johanna Rohan
Designed by Stella Vassiliou
Series Design by James Lowe
Illustrations by Boris Silvestri
Production Controller Seona Galbally
Photo Research by Michelle Cottrill
Audio recordings by Juliet Hill, Picture Start
Spoken by Matthew King and Abbe Holmes
Printed in China by 1010 Printing International Ltd

Website www.nelsonthornes.com

Acknowledgements
The author and publisher would like to acknowledge permission to reproduce material from
the following sources:
Photographs by AAP Image/ Jim Baynes, p. 23 top; The Art Archive, p. 22/ Musée des Beaux Arts Troyes/
Dagli Orti, p. 21; Corbis/ epa/ Richard Lewis, p. 7/ Michael Maslan Historic Photographs, p. 8; Getty Images,/
AFP/ Attila Kisbenedek, p. 6; Newsphotos, p. 4/ Guy Thayer, p. 5; Photolibrary/ The Bridgeman Art Library,
front cover, pp. 1, 23 bottom/ The Print Collector, p. 20/ Mary Evans Picture Library, p. 9.

THE BEGINNINGS OF DEMOCRACY

NICOLAS BRASCH

Contents

Chapter 1	**Defining Democracy**	4
Chapter 2	**The Ancient Greeks**	8
Chapter 3	**The Ancient Romans**	16
Chapter 4	**The Spread of Democracy**	20
Glossary and Index		24

Chapter 1

DEFINING DEMOCRACY

Democracy is a system of **government**. It involves members of a community having a say in the way they are governed.

However, the amount of involvement people can have in the way they are governed differs a lot.

A true democracy would give
every person in a community
the right to vote on every issue.
This form of democracy
would be difficult in practice,
because it would take too long for decisions
to be made.
It would only work well in a small community.

Today, a democracy usually involves people voting for others to **represent** them.

The **representatives** then make decisions on behalf of the community, instead of every member of a community voting on every issue.

This form of government is called a representative democracy.

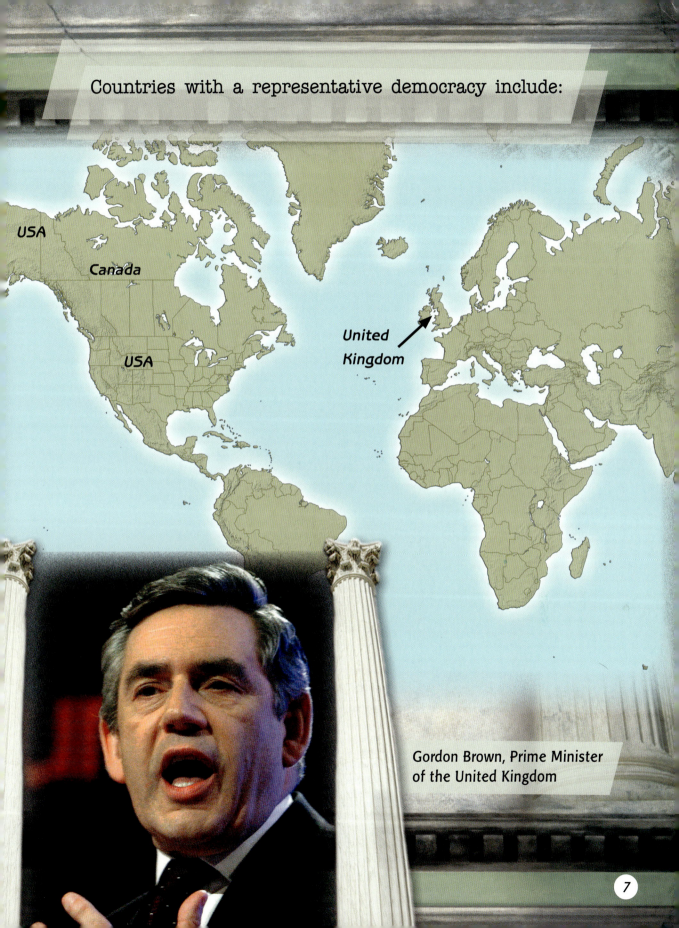

Countries with a representative democracy include:

Gordon Brown, Prime Minister of the United Kingdom

Chapter 2

THE ANCIENT GREEKS

The word democracy comes from the Greek language.

It is believed that the ancient Greeks were the first people to form **democratic societies** about 2600 years ago.

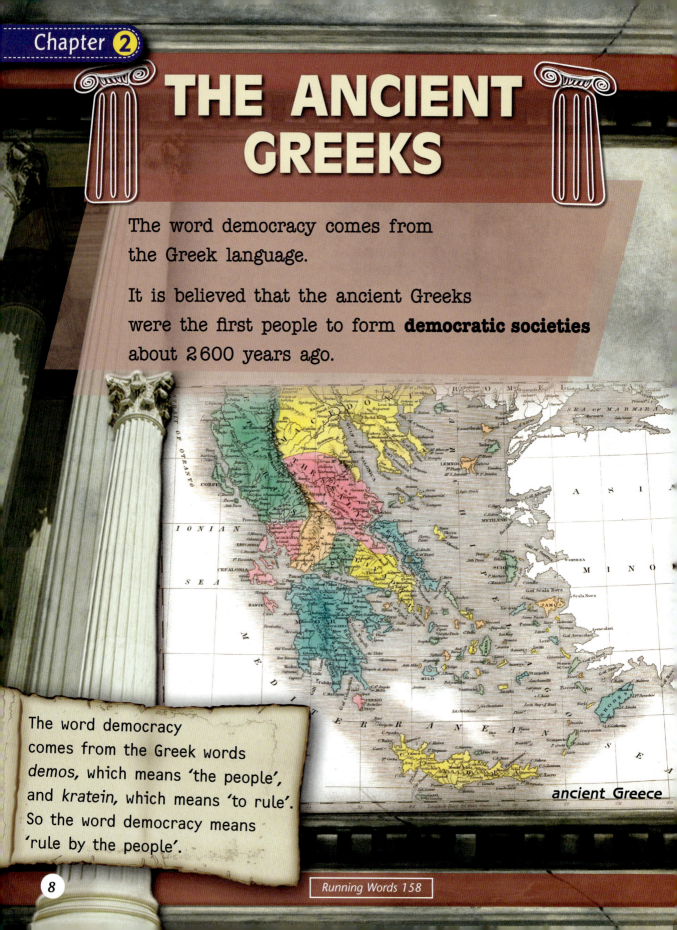

ancient Greece

The word democracy comes from the Greek words *demos*, which means 'the people', and *kratein*, which means 'to rule'. So the word democracy means 'rule by the people'.

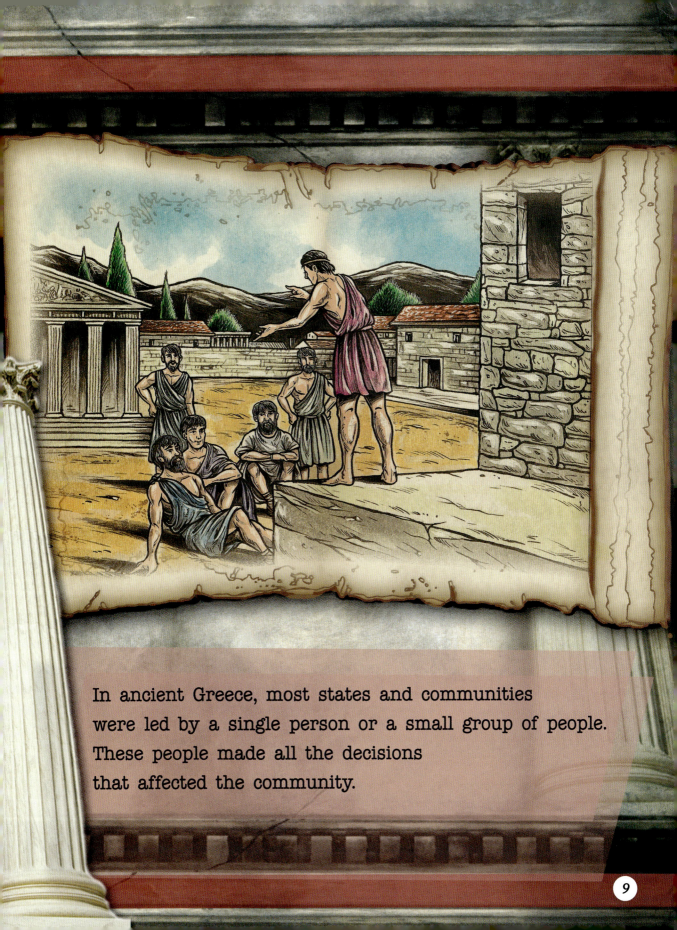

In ancient Greece, most states and communities were led by a single person or a small group of people. These people made all the decisions that affected the community.

But, the Greeks decided this system was unfair. So they thought up fairer ways for decisions to be made.

The ancient Greeks came up with a system of government where the country was split into small states.

All the male citizens in the states voted on important issues.

The Greeks then elected representatives from these states who formed a government.

The role of the representatives was to ensure that the decisions made by the citizens were carried out.

The representatives could not make their own laws.

This democratic system worked well in ancient Greece for two main reasons.

First, ancient Greece was quite small.

The ancient Greeks were able to create small states with no more than 10 000 people in them.

This made democratic decision-making possible.

Second, this system of democracy worked well in ancient Greece because the Greeks limited the type of people who could vote.

Women weren't allowed to have a say in decision-making.

Slaves weren't allowed to have a say in decision-making, either.

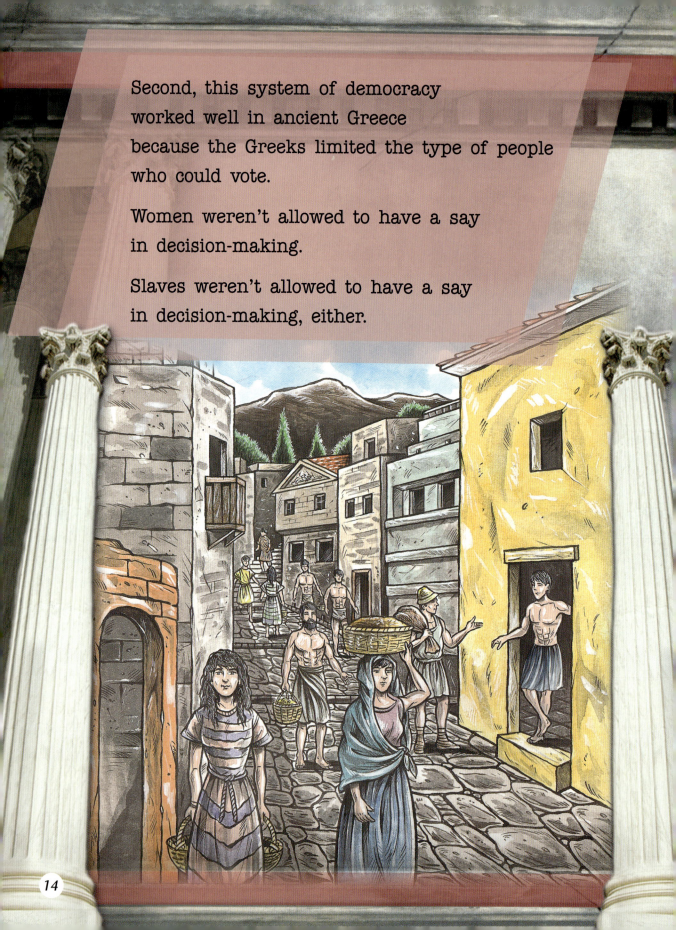

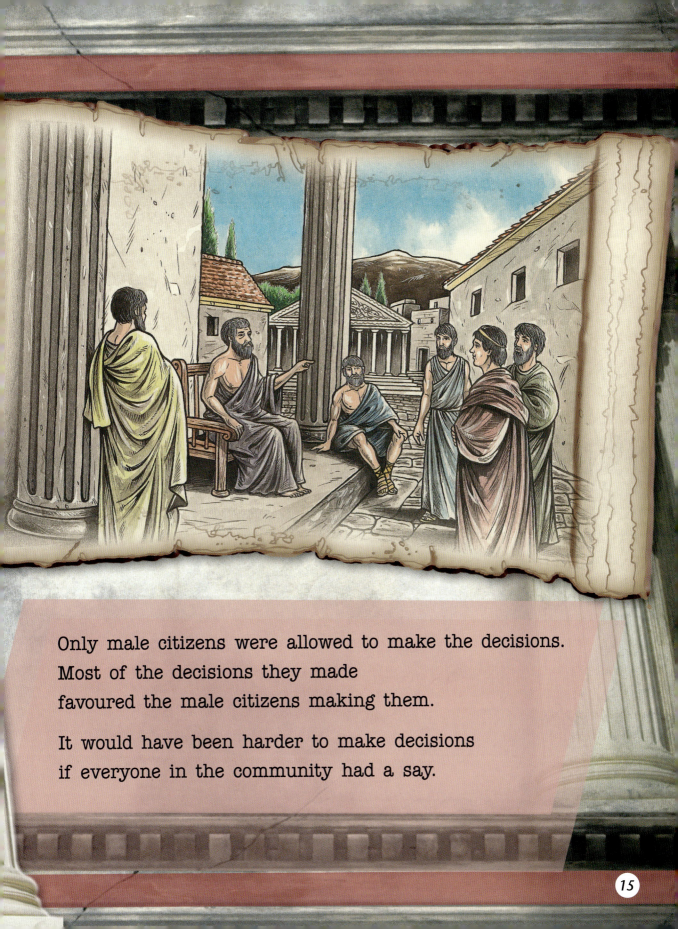

Only male citizens were allowed to make the decisions. Most of the decisions they made favoured the male citizens making them.

It would have been harder to make decisions if everyone in the community had a say.

Chapter 3
THE ANCIENT ROMANS

The ancient Romans took some aspects of Greek democracy and formed their own democratic systems.

Ancient Roman democracy was closer to modern representative democracy than the ancient Greek version.

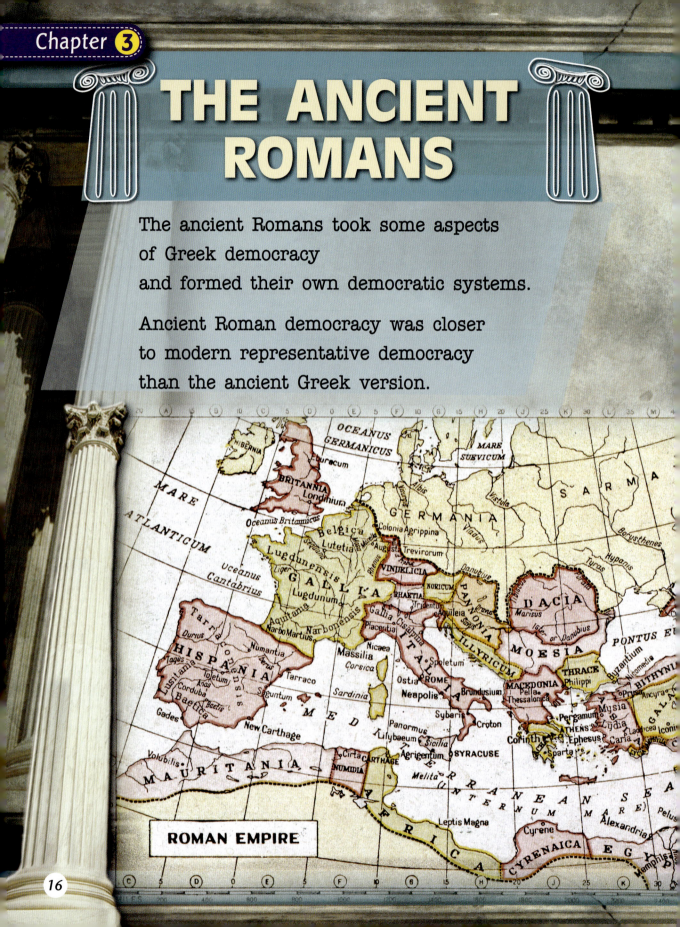

ROMAN EMPIRE

Instead of giving men the right to vote on individual issues, the Roman system allowed men to elect other men to represent them in a government.

The elected representatives then made the decisions.

Like the Greek form of democracy, the Roman version only involved men.

In addition, wealthy men had more representatives in government than poor men.

So, most of the decisions made in ancient Rome favoured wealthy men.

Chapter 4

THE SPREAD OF DEMOCRACY

When the **Roman Empire** ended about 1600 years ago, democracy nearly ended as well.

Apart from a few small states in Europe, countries around the world were ruled by individuals or small groups.

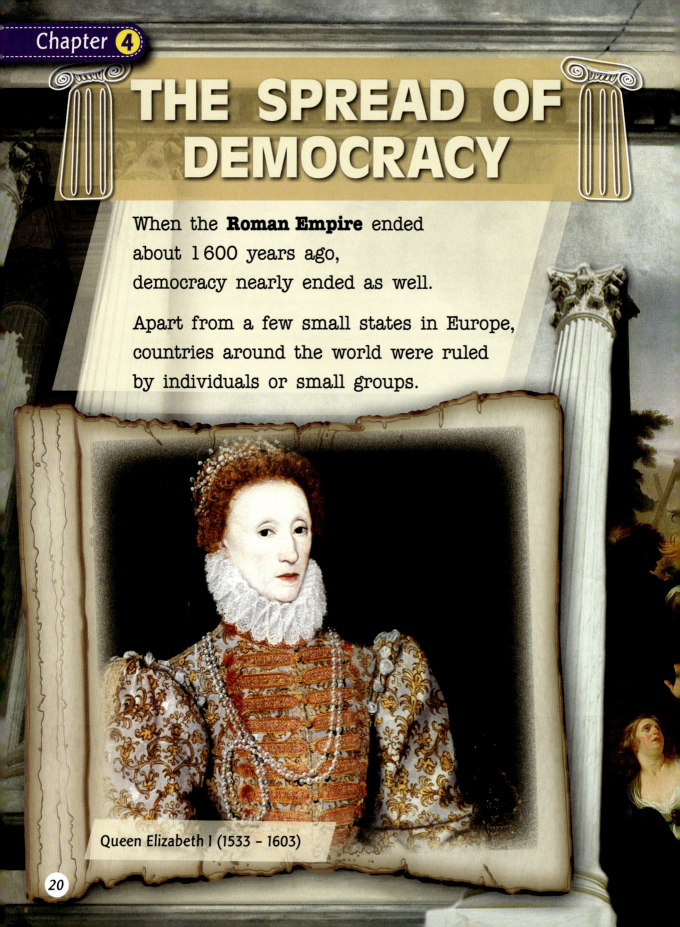

Queen Elizabeth I (1533 – 1603)

For the next 1200 years, not much changed.

But, by the 1600s, the people in several European countries started to rise up against their leaders.

the French people rise up against Édouard Molé, cardinal of Bayeux, in 1648

In 1649, King Charles I of England became the first major ruler in Europe to be overthrown.

He was tried for **treason**, found guilty and beheaded.

The execution of King Charles I led to the formation of an English government based on democratic ideas.

Other European countries followed, including France.

However, these new democratic nations didn't extend the idea of democracy to the countries they **colonised**.

These colonies had to fight for their own democratic governments. In some cases, they fought until the end of the 20th century.

Independence day celebrations in the Solomon Islands

the House of Commons, England, 19th century

Glossary

colonised	set up control over a foreign land
democratic societies	communities supporting and embracing democracy
government	the ruling body of a country or state
represent	to act or speak for people
representatives	people chosen to act or speak for other people
Roman Empire	the empire under Roman rule, from 27 BC to 395 AD
treason	the crime of betraying your country

Index

ancient Greece 8–15

ancient Rome 16–19

Brown, Gordon 7

Charles I, King of England 22

male citizens 15

Rome Empire 20

slaves 14

women 14